The Plural of Happiness

Selected Poems of Herman de Coninck

Translated by Laure-Anne Bosselaar and Kurt Brown
Foreword by Charles Simic

Oberlin College Press
Oberlin, Ohio

The FIELD Translation Series, Volume 28
Oberlin College Press, 50 N. Professor St., Oberlin, OH 44074
www.oberlin.edu/ocpress

Library of Congress Cataloging-in-Publication Data

Coninck, Herman de.
    [Poems. English. Selections]
    The plural of happiness : selected poems of Herman de Coninck
/ translated by Laure-Anne Bosselaar and Kurt Brown ; foreword
by Charles Simic.
        p. cm. — (Field translation series ; v. 28)
    ISBN-13: 978-0-932440-30-3 (pbk. : alk. paper)
    ISBN-10: 0-932440-30-4 (pbk. : alk. paper)
    1. Coninck, Herman de—Translations into English.   I. Bosselaar,
Laure-Anne, 1943- . II. Brown, Kurt. III. Title.
PT6466.13.O5A2 2006
839.31'164—dc22
                                    2006023082

Cover painting: Fritz van den Berghe, "La Présence Perpétuelle," from the private collection of Dr. H. van Kerckhove, Hasselt, Belgium.
Cover and book design: Steve Farkas.

The Plural of Happiness

Selected Poems of Herman de Coninck

This is for you, Kristien,
and in memory of Herman

Contents

From *Fingerprints* (1997)

Foreword

What a bunch of boring provincials we would all be without translations from other languages! Left alone, homegrown literatures are rarely adventurous. They thrive on repetition, happy to write the same poem over and over in the foolish expectation that the old tricks will work again. Reading this book, I was reminded of the obvious: there was no important American poet in the last hundred years that had not benefited by straying outside of our native tradition. Even Frost, who may seem so insular, so much a local product, knew well the old Roman poets. Translators are our great, unacknowledged teachers. They enrich our literature by providing examples of other sensibilities, other ways of writing a story or a poem. They also make literary discoveries. Someone we have never heard of before becomes a familiar name and a model. For us who love literature, the hunch that there may be great poets and writers out there who have not yet been translated is an absolute torment. All we can do is hope and wait for someone to get around to translating them.

Years before I read his marvelous poems, I had heard Herman de Coninck praised in Belgium and Holland. He was an extraordinary love poet with a huge following, I was told, but not knowing Dutch, I had no idea what to expect. As a rule, one tends to be on one's guard when it comes to love poetry. So much of it is embarrassing, one can understand why many greatly accomplished and wide-ranging poets never wrote any. There's no quicker way of making a complete ass of oneself. It's the skewed nature of experience, of course, that makes it hard to relate. Love is a form of blindness and even madness, we've been rightly told. "The lover loves the body as if it were the soul and the soul as if it were the body," Octavio Paz says. None of us is very good at making sense of our infatuations. Is there anybody more foolish than a lover trying to explain his or her love? The vocabulary is so limited, so hackneyed—and yet, unfortunately, there's no other. A poem that succeeds in recalling what it meant to be in love is a utopian project. It can't be done, one thinks, and yet, the impossible sometimes occurs. There are great love poems among the literatures of the world, and some of them have been written, it turns out, by the Belgian poet Herman de Coninck.

The poems in *The Plural of Happiness* are by and large very short. Their subject frequently is some moment of intense feeling, erotic excitement, happiness or sorrow. Time is the perennial enemy of lovers. So much happens in so brief a time, no wonder his poems often read like elegies. "A poet must work hard learning to be silent," he says in a poem called "Ars Poetica." It is the silence that reminds the poet of the poverty of words to express the deepest emotions. Reticence, the fear of not saying it right, becomes part of the drama in these poems. The less de Coninck says, the more his poems engage our imagination. "See how Melinda sleeps holding / her breasts in her arms like two blond / children," he writes in one. Erotic poems tend to obliterate the object of their passion in that we rarely get any idea of the other person beyond her sensual attributes. Not here. All of de Coninck's women have their own recognizable and distinct identities. It's not just his own love that interests him; their experience matters to him and has him worried and mystified.

Translating poems of such brevity and mastery is a difficult undertaking. Short lyric poems are the hardest to translate because such poems don't have much of a narrative and because the little that happens in them is already about the inability of language to convey the richness of experience. It's not just the idiomatic language, the formal concision, but the many intangibles that one has to translate. One is obliged to take into account not only what is said, but also what is intentionally left out. A good translation is a miracle of nature. Against all odds, it manages to include both. Reading this book, I was amazed again and again by the skill of Bosselaar and Brown. They are both fine poets in their own right and that helps a great deal. They make it hard to imagine that these strange, original, and absolutely fabulous poems were written in any other language but English.

Charles Simic

Translators' Introduction

Herman de Coninck, who was born in 1944 and died in 1997, is Flanders' most renowned poet. His work, sewn with puns, double entendres, unconventional rhymes and syntax in concise, intricate forms, presents the translator with formidable problems. How to represent such linguistic acrobatics, how to preserve the formal grace and delicate wit without losing the lightness of touch, the deftness of thought, the quips and jabs that mark his poetry?

De Coninck loved the sonnet and was fascinated by the form, translating many of Edna St. Vincent Millay's sonnets into Dutch. Like Millay, one of de Coninck's major subjects was love, the intimate sexual and psychological relations that exist between men and women. This is not an easy subject for a contemporary writer to undertake. After centuries of love poetry, many poets have attested to the difficulty of writing freshly about love in modern times. The problem, simply stated, is: how to avoid the clichés and platitudes, the shopworn strategies and gestures of the past? De Coninck's solution is the playfulness and technical skill he brings to his writing, a way of both honoring and escaping the pitfalls of his subject.

So, for instance, in "The way you came in and said hello," language itself is used as a metaphor for physical seduction. This seems appropriate, since poetry has often been regarded as a form of seduction, albeit an imaginative one. And form, as in the best poems, becomes an extension of content—here in a most charming and enjoyable way. The long middle stanza is contained within a parenthesis, which contains in its turn the erotic trope "you opened your parentheses, I entered…." The poem hinges on what happens within the intimate, discreet confines of that parenthesis, and it's doubtful that de Coninck missed the coy, labial image suggested by the opposing curves of those elegant parentheses either.

In the poem "Hérault," a difficult wordplay occurs in the last stanza which is all but impossible to recreate in English. Here is what the stanza looks like in Dutch:

En je weet: ik heb niet wat ik heb.
De branding van de wind
waait een zee van tijd zacht heen
en weer. Het is eb.

The English reader will notice immediately the rhyme at the end of lines one and four of this stanza. In Dutch, this is extremely important to the overall effect of the poem. What de Coninck says, literally, in line one is: "I have not what I have," or—in proper English syntax—"I do not have what I have." In the last sentence of the poem, de Coninck writes: "It is ebb." But the delicate play of sound between "heb" and "heb" in line one, and "Het" and "eb" in line four is lost in English, except for the very distant, almost undetectable resonance between the English words "have" and "ebb." But there's more: the "H" in line four is close enough to the final word "eb" to resonate slightly with the verbs in line one. We can see it visually ("**H**et is **eb**"). What he means to suggest by this soundplay is that the Dutch reader hear "It is ebb(ing)" and "It is having" at the same time. That is: what de Coninck *has* is this moment in the Hérault, which is instantly receding, blown away by and into the ocean of time. De Coninck plays with sound in similar ways throughout his work.

Although he is best known as a writer of charming and witty love poems, de Coninck is also a poet of considerable seriousness and power when writing about war, history, and human mortality. Born during the second world war, he was too young to have experienced the occupation of Belgium first-hand. But the wounds of that occupation haunted his childhood, and the evidence of that violent incursion lay all about him as he was growing up in the post-war period. De Coninck is sometimes a darkly ironic, somberly truthful observer of human experience. This is apparent in poems like "In the Seaport of Oostduinkerke," where he reflects: "To die, and fetch the papers they would soon fill, / men were good at that..." while women had humbler things to do: "Just be there, to see what remains alive" after the fighting stops.

De Coninck's understanding of war is conditioned by his knowledge of how people live and act in the world, how psychological imperatives and social roles may trap us in inevitable, self-destructive fates. These truths may appear in his work like shadows of the sunnier self who goes around quipping and making love.

Another of de Coninck's themes is family and fatherhood. Scattered throughout his seven books of poetry are poems that address not only his own children but also himself as a son and a husband. Reading these chronologically, over the course of his career, one is able to detect the faint outlines of a narrative, or at the very least a life filled, like all lives, with moments of discovery, change, and tragedy. We have tried to represent this "narrative" with a sprinkling of poems which might allow the reader to follow the story, if only occasionally and at a distance. Our choices of what to include from each book were also guided by our sense of which poems might be possible to translate successfully, as well as by our desire to represent, as well as we could, a clear picture of de Coninck's strengths and obsessions as a writer.

Beginning with *Lithe Love* in 1969, de Coninck produced seven full-length books of poetry up to and including his last collection, *Fingerprints*, which was published posthumously in 1997. Poems from each of these collections appear here, and the order of the books has been maintained. But we have sometimes re-arranged the sequence of poems from their original order in each book, both to allow the poems to speak to each other more effectively, and to allow the "narrative" mentioned above to emerge more clearly.

Before his untimely death in 1997, we had the great privilege of working on a number of these poems personally with Herman—sometimes over the phone to Belgium, sometimes by the use of the fax machine, and once at our home in Snowmass, Colorado, where Herman was a guest at the Aspen Writers' Conference. But a particularly happy time occurred when we were visiting Paris and Herman and his wife Kristien took the train down from Brussels to meet us. Herman was most helpful and encouraging, telling us that he wished we would always choose sense over the strictures and rigidities of language and form. That is: he wanted the poems to sound like real poems in American English, not ungainly transliterations of the Dutch. If this meant taking some liberties with the originals, well, we were not to hesitate but do the best we could. Herman's face lit up when we promised him we would.

Laure-Anne Bosselaar and Kurt Brown

from *Lithe Love* (1969)

"I come from far away"

I come from far away
from where you were beautiful behind your hair
as an island behind reeds.
And your mouth fell, slow, slowly
over my face like
night over land, like silence
over this poem.

How pale my hands are
since then, as if to be put in a shrine:

in the illusion that we are still together.

"The way you came in and said hello"

The way you came in and said hello
and stepped out of your clothes, your words

(the next-to-last you took
off was the word "darling,"
and the last a smile; then
you opened your parentheses, I entered,
and you closed them)

was how you left, slipped
on a few flimsy words
of good-bye
and shivered.

"What a lack of pathos"

What a lack of pathos
the way he says: "Hello.
So you no longer love me."
And she, getting rid of a last
sandwich bite: "No."
And he, he goes on talking
to the phone until it says *click*,
as though it were swallowing something.

"Will I be unable to shut up"

Will I be unable to shut up about
your legs that welcomed me with
open arms?

Or shall I tell you about a distant king
whose thoughts of you are changed
into the moon by a magician?

And will my hands lie on your breasts
as softly as snow on the
most beautiful mountains I've ever seen?

Yes.

"When the sun shouts golden orders"

When the sun shouts golden orders
and squads of wild white flowers
ride toward summer wars,

Eva jumps off mountains
whirling laughter around herself
like a lasso.

Will she wear her joy
the way soft buttocks wear
sheer panties?

Yes, and she will be absolutely
forbidden: a paradise
inside the gates of her name.

"And she hugged him with all her sins"

And she hugged him with all her sins
and mouths. And she kissed him
with her nights, with all her forevers.
Where did she come up with all those things?
He walked through her words
as through a soft rain, and couldn't live anywhere
else in the world, he wandered in love.
And she taught him to be unable
to say what he felt—but to feel.
How many legs did she throw around him
and how many snakes?
And how long did she take to tell a lie,
saying the word *beloved*?

It took months—that word was many months long.

"Fat-assed. Settling into the power"

Fat-assed. Settling into the power
of his enormous body as into an armchair:
the yellow Buddha, the sun.
Small breezes struggle towards his throne,
like devotees, but
he waves them away,
he wants to *eat*:
huge meadows lie steaming
like hot plates.

How different from the girls
whom I lie down with on manicured lawns
to nibble chocolates, or in high grasses
to sip diminutives:
their shrill voices like dots on i's,
their tittering
like fawns in loud forests of laughter.
So much quicker at doting
than love.

"Smack in the heart of July"

Smack in the heart of July
I came across you. I live here, you said.
I was watching the flowers. Yes, I see that,
I said, and where did you learn the art
of not lasting? Here also, you said.

You were lithe, and your words so
transparent: I saw you entirely
through them.
There I was, already lying in the grass,
and what did I hold in my hand?
A little ear, into which I poured the long word
darlingest, without spilling.

Sailor's Song

See how Melinda sleeps holding
her breasts in her arms like two blond
children. And not far away
sleeps her oldest—with the black
curls. Why would Melinda
want children? Her body
is a whole family.

"What a great idea of her parents"

What a great idea of her parents
to produce Melinda. No wonder
all she wanted to study in college
was herself. A science called
psychology, I think. In no time at all
she just wanted to be pretty
and meet me.

Look at what I have here, she says,
leading me to the window: all kinds
of things to study.
And look at what else I have, she says,
pointing to herself: it can kiss, she adds
from atop her long legs
and I feel my happy ending grow.

"Your sweaters"

Your sweaters, your red and white
scarves, your stockings and panties
("Made with love" says the label)
and your bras (there's poetry in those things,
especially when you wear them)
are scattered around this poem
as they are around your room.

Come in, reader, make yourself
comfortable, don't trip over
the messy syntax and kicked-off shoes,
have a seat.

(Meanwhile, we kiss between these parentheses,
so the reader won't see us) How do you
like this window on reality?
All you see here exists. Isn't that exactly
how it is in a poem?

"Half the time during the day, I slept"

Half the time during the day, I slept
in sun and grass. So I'd be rested at night
to sleep with you.

You lived a free, godless life
like women in France.
I came in, said hello.
You didn't even look up, saying
if you want a beer, go
get it yourself in the cellar.

And later, remember how your body
rolled and quivered beneath me like a pleasure boat?
Sometimes you'd sigh a contented, extended "mmm"
like a motor I kept softly running.

from *As Long As Snow Remains* (1975)

After an Argument

It all depends on how you look at it:
we stand as close to each other—
or as far—as two mountain peaks.
(You're the Jungfrau.)

Nice weather, I say.
Words that float towards you
like a gondola

over the clouds.

Poetry

When you bury yourself in the sheets, sulking,
you actually mean: come lie by me.

When you slam the door and run,
you actually mean: come get me.

And when you say: "I love you"
you mean: "Do you love me?"

Do you see now that poetry is necessary,
for if I said "Yes,"
it wouldn't mean a thing.

Elephant

He's made of the grossest stuff,
wears his pants like Bozo the Clown,
grubby knees, strutting around
like aunt Bertha who drives a tango into the ground sans grace
while his ass, puckering, reminds you of dentures

that were just removed. And then his trunk
right between the eyes. How would you look
if they stuck your dick in the middle of your face?

The Rhinoceros

He's as thick
as a redneck.

He's like the 20th Century
B.C., that suddenly stands up in history
and takes a little step
forwards,
he can't do much more.

He's made of slumping concrete,
as solemn as tenements collapsing
in slow motion, that's how
he sits, lies down,

ponders his inner being
as empty as a bunker
in which there have been no soldiers
since '44.

Triangle

It was a good triangle:
I loved you
and myself.

I loved you like
the first time: as if each time
were the last.

I loved the way I got you
into all kinds of states,
Belgium, France, Holland, Yugoslavia,
happiness was indeed as wide as whole countries
and every one different from the last.

I loved you for the way,
reading over my shoulder, you'd say:
yeah, yeah, write as well as you can,
that's easy, but show me what else you can do.

And I loved myself,
for how heavenly it was
to be me
in your arms.

Study in Color

And the black crow came
flying from above seven mountains
bringing a letter in its beak:

a black envelope with a black
card inside, on which, written in white,
was the word "black."

Death's night is that dark,
our fear that bleak.

Birthday Poem

You never said anything. I always had to ask
if you loved me. You just kissed me.
When I asked if it was safe that first time
you kissed me once more. And afterwards, if I had loved you just so,
you kissed me again, o.

You never said a thing, you spoke only with your eyes.
Your eyes, completely alone,
abandoned in your face when I left you;
your eyes after crying:
you weren't there any longer,
you gazed at me from a long way off
and I had to journey there.

And when I had made that journey
the eyes with which you said "darling"
watched to see if the word lost something
on its way to me.
And when you were lying in the meadow
by the side of the road,
almost all of you broken,
your legs, your ribs, your eyes, me,
you never said a thing, you spoke only with your gaze,
as you were lying there...
eyeing me, dying.

And those eyes that your son has now
with which he says: don't leave—
you never said it, he says it, and it's you
staring at me through his eyes.

from *With a Sound of Hobo* (1980)

Defuser of Mines

No, this wasn't love, it was too full of danger.
My hands that carefully reached, reached
for your breast, like hands of a mine defuser.

It wasn't love, it was both larger and smaller.
As large as your breast and as small
as your nipple, small as your mouth, silent crater,

large as the laughing mouth of a stranger.
As large as the stroking, already
wanting to heal the pain that comes later.

And as small as you wanted that pain to be.

For Each Other

Then I loved only your eyes.
Now also the crow's feet around them.
Just as an old word, like *compassion*,
has more in it than a new word. Before, there was only haste

to have what one had, over and over.
Then there was only now. Now there's also then.
There's more to love.
And more ways to love it.

Even doing nothing is one of them.
Just sitting here together with a book.
Or not together, in the café around the corner.

Or not seeing each other for a few days
and missing each other. But always each other,
now almost seven years after all.

Hérault

Evening in the Hérault. The scent of thyme
floats heavy on the air. No need to go anywhere.
It hangs in this valley, like us,
the way you'd like to drift, no matter where,

as long as it's here. Mist carefully
hovers over this land, the way
one doesn't touch a sleeping child,
breathing over it.

I don't really have what I have.
Waves of wind blow an ocean of time
softly, back and forth.
It is ebbing.

Time Out

Once upon a time, in childhood games,
if a shoelace was untied,
one could say "Time out" and be
safe, out of the game for awhile.

For you that rule should have remained.
If only you had said "Time out, I've just
lost my husband," then the last ten years wouldn't count.

As if, instead of dying,
you were just playing hide-and-seek
and we still
hadn't found you.

Two Kinds of Nothing

Luxury is the difference between
driving a car without a radio
and driving with the car radio off.

Silence is the difference between
saying nothing and having said it all.
Or between a regular silence and the silence
remaining after the last line
of a poem about silence.

She and He

She bravely holds
her happiness up—
and her breasts. Her temper's
wired like a bra.

He's composed of joyful
ha-ha's, but for years
he's locked his passion behind bars:
the stripes of his pajamas.

Mother

What you do with time
is what a grandmother clock
does with it: strike twelve
and take its time doing it.
You're the clock: time passes,
you remain. And wait.

Waiting is what happens to
a snow-covered garden,
a trunk under moss,
hope for better times
in the nineteenth century,
or words in a poem.

For poetry is about letting things
grow moldy together, like grapes
turning into wine, reality into preserves,
and hoarding words
in the cellar of yourself.

from *The Acres of Memory* (1985)

Genesis

It was the sixth day. Adam was ready.
He saw the oaks firmly rooted
in the void. Power is a matter of branching.
He had seen the mountains, vast storerooms holding
only themselves, high empty cellars.
And deer. With legs as thin as stethoscopes
they stood listening to the breast of the earth,
and as soon as they heard something, they ran away,
inventing pizzicato as they fled the horizon.
And he had seen the sea, the busy swelling and receding
that makes one calm. And the empty, provocative gestures
of the wind, *come along, come along*, though no one followed.
And the depths, gulfs that make one uneasy. And being silent,
because that's what everything was doing, and being too big.
Then God said: and now you. No, said Adam.

"He had hoped it could be done without autumn"

He had hoped it could be done without autumn.
Sudden snow. Ascetic white. Precise cold.
Less thinking about its significance,
more attention to the healing from it—

and get it over with. Not this months-long
stripping of dead boughs, the sorting out,
cleaning up, such endless unraveling of loss
it makes him want to go re-hang leaves on every branch.

Without bitterness, he had hoped it could be done.
But the whole garden rots from hourly blasts
of rain, then seethes from a minute of sun.
Oh, if everything could just expire, and nothing needed to last.

"If only he could, just like that, leave her"

If only he could, just like that, leave her
for another country, another I, another wife—
but if he did, he'd only leave himself behind.
He was tender, like a little boy whose whining

she endured, who constantly
complained about their petty problems,
until finally he'd grow silent, shedding happy
tears, a wrinkled man of eighty in her arms.

In ancient times there was a legend that averred
she-bears licked their shapeless newborn cubs
into their bear shape. That's how carefully

they nuzzle each other.
She gives him his "I" shape
then strokes him into her.

In the Seaport of Oostduinkerke

The instant I wake up it starts: women and children
first! Because the men are hung over, through
with talking world politics until dawn.
They're drained from that, and the bottles too.

There was a time when men went to war
for a couple of years to mingle with others
of their kind, although all that dying got to be a bore.
(Where's daddy? There, behind that historical gesture.)

To die, and fetch the papers they would soon fill,
men were good at that. And later, star in other people's
tales. Women do humbler things with time to kill:

Just be there, to see what remains alive.
Or change something (clothes, a husband).
Let the bombs drop. Continue to survive.

Glass Shards in the Sun

in Memoriam Matris

He steps into the room as carefully
as into a new century.
Still as snow on snow,
her hands lie on the back
of the turned sheet.
She's silent as a fist
that won't open again. She stares at him.
He hears her smile crack.

*

One night, between two heart attacks, she
quickly tells him where to find the key to her safe.
He had imagined a more poignant line for the end of her life.

She knows him better. Dying is nothing, but all
that paperwork one inherits! "You keep busy with acquiring,
I with expiring."

What do you call something you are no longer? An ex-son?
An ache? The door by which he entered life is open. There's a draft
of infinity. Of finity. He must remain. She's gone.

*

Even while you were still alive, a slow crumbling
took place, took more and more of you: mumbling,
prayerful, your mouth like a river
on a 3D map, with lots of tributaries.

Your flesh shrank, pulled away from your teeth
in a ghastly smile. Your hands hovered inches above
objects, uncertain if it was still worth moving
things around. Your mouth opened like a 0

as if it wanted to express what your life
had been: 0 on a scale of 10.
And those eyes of yours, thin as the eyes of needles,
kept watching.

*

Niagara Falls, Mt. Everest, the Grand Canyon
pictures on your calendar at home.
You called it nature's art, but it was
the opposite of that, what is left of the earth

after suffering erosion for millennia,
glacial ice and wind: unable to be anything
other than what finally remains:
hard, cold stone.

Under the photo of the Dolomites I read:
"The Dolomites owe their jagged profile
to the rock they are made of,
namely dolomite."
That's true also for your face:
it owes its etched, strict peace—
your mouth a scar of what had to be

almost surgically removed:
your constant gab—to what kept on
resisting. Pride. Stubbornness. Sorrow.

*

The Grand Canyon. Ten million years of erosion.
The heart is worn away like that too. What's left is what you
no longer have. A character full of rocky
outcroppings. Like the k sounds of "cataract":

kilometers of ocher angles through which
time dives like a horizontal waterfall. Here time is
simply endless and everywhere:

corridors of thought leading to the void, through
prehistoric passions of water scooping out
absence. An eighteen-carat jewel
under the sun. And what remains after all this passion:
lots of space.

*

I only have two kinds of photographs where you smile:
with your children, up to about eight years old;
then with your grandchildren (the eldest is thirteen
and not yet brash).

What happened between those epochs is explained
on five neatly labeled homeopathic vials
in your medicine chest: "Fear," "Depression" (twice),
"Acute Anxiety," "Panic Attacks." The dramatic

battle of three daily drops each against an ocean.
You went on being a teacher. A bully of a woman.
"Twenty years of little daily losses are better
than losing everything at once," you reasoned.

And so you laughed again, holding one of those tots
in your arms—after all that hugeness in your life.
That's how you appear in your daughter's wedding shots.
Rigid with back-pain, clean as a crooked spike

that's been hammered straight again. And you
laugh. After the deaths of your one best friend,
your husband, brothers, sisters—as if this wouldn't end—

like glass shards laughing in the sun.

*

On the page of a little notebook, what your grandson said:
"'I'm four years old? Wait, I need to think hard about that.' Then
he bellyflops into a big chair, chin on the armrest,
face towards the floor."

You kept track of the oddest things. Just as I did,
eight years later, when he answered you: "I only realize now
all you did for me. You spoiled me
when I was with you. Also, you loved me a lot."

How beautiful that "also."
All you did was love him—but in a hundred
different ways. Also in your notebook:
"Hope is the same as the roads

in this flat country. There isn't a road
until hordes of people trudge the same way,
and the road creates itself." And you must have thought:
"This also happens if only one person treks the same way over and
    over."

Like you towards him.

*

I wish I could be a little sick again,
so that you could bring me a cup of hot tea
with rum for each one of me—

whoever I felt like being—
the little milquetoast, or the brave stoic,
incurable and happily sick.

You'd always explain, lay things out
then place the answers back inside my head.
I only had to close my eyes to understand.

How much you're gone, now that you're gone.
How much room there is.
How much less sadness.

Your skin is transparent as a glass
from which you drank the last drop:
yourself. And I, who wasn't there to clasp

your living hands, your ten gray
fingers, because you were so distant, so very
distant. I finally held them as you slipped away.

*

Where do events go
when they're done happening here?

Where do shreds of fog blow
after they have left this place clear,

leaving all exposed? Where will snow
snow, and not lose a single flake

but leave everything as it is, just so?
Have words a home when they're no longer

able to describe your face,
now finally gone?

How will your half-open mouth
become this poem?

.

*

Autumn. Half-starved grass.
Thistles survive, denial
remains, few words pass
into language
or make it on their own.
It's work to hack away,
until from all the facts
only two numbers
remain—on stone.

from *Singular* (1991)

"For six years she learned what lasting was"

For six years she learned what lasting was:
what parents did, and thus what everything would do:
a chair with a table, now with then.
The plural of happiness was: us.

Since then she has learned what singular is:
she. Today half of you, tomorrow half of me.

When she was eight she was ten.
One half of her face sweet,
the other sweeter. Scared to choose
between to lose and to lose.

Today she is simply twelve.
Four parents: two real, two step.
She can't sleep without endless kissing.
She always wins. She has learned what lasting is.
What parents don't, but children do.

"'Yes, sleep,' I say"

"Yes, sleep," I say
to a daughter who's been asleep for awhile
and wakes up.

Thunder cracks. Maybe I'd like her
to be afraid, then I could be her daddy.
But what can I do with her but
do nothing.

It's like words. Things happen.
They'd happen just the same without words.
But without words then.

"She has all she needs for kissing"

She has all she needs for kissing, two arms for my neck,
and to top it all off, herself, to tussle around with.
She has twenty questions but only two eyes,
which do what a question mark does with a line,

or what her mother did wearing new clothes. Sashaying,
that might work.
May she sleep with me? She tries a wink—
(if four eyes don't work, three might).

Later when I whisper against her,
"It's nice and warm here,"
she answers in her sleep: "That's
especially for you."

On a Picture by Dre Peeters

What remains of a man is an ape:
me and my balls, the three
of us. Look, little balls.

What remains of an ape is a man,
as dead as I'll have to be,
sweet brother, wise-ass Mongolian,
little monk, eyeless snout.

What remains of a man are teeth
behind which he's dead.
And a back behind which it's written

how love became his opponent
and eternity a moment.

"Just as this island belongs to the gulls"

Just as this island belongs to the gulls
and the gulls to their cry
and their cry to the wind
and the wind to no one,

so is this island the gulls
and the gulls are their cry
and their cry is the wind
and the wind is no one's.

"Once, a fist hit the table"

Once, a fist hit the table
of this country and remained there:
a castle.

He lives nowhere,
because it's no different here than anywhere else:
there are walls around
but it's still nowhere.

It's also no home or life.
It's wanting nothing
and doing it here.

Everything is too heavy in this house.
Wind blows hard on the hearth,
flames bark like dogs.

And next to the fire sits
a silent man who searched for himself
and, alas, has found him.

Juniper Tree, Canyonlands

Ten specks of dust and a crack
are enough for him to shoot roots into rock.
So he hangs there, as cocked
and crooked as he is big.

And that's O.K. because he's already dead,
and he can keep that up forever.
He stands there like Zadkine's
Orpheus playing harp
on wooden strings, old
and mad with soundlessness.

With too many arms, too slowly, just too *too*.
But branching with willing despair.

Here

Not much is needed to love here.
Someone says "here" against the unmeasurable.

A coin on the mantle,
a passport photo. The unforgettable
is that small.

Yonder

I'm looking for a village.
And in that a house. And in that a
room, where there's a bed, where there's a woman.
And on that woman, a lap.

Outside the river broadens
to go farther, the silver-scaled,
fish-rich, boat-carrying,
sea-seeking, ever-remaining one.

So a comparison seeks
a poem for the night,
a man a lover,
a bookmark a gutter.
Night snaps the book shut.

from *Breaststroke* (1994)

1958

1.

My uncle is dead. I get to go to the funeral
with my mother. Rarely have I been so *hers.*
Afterwards, coffee, pastries, funeral party, the great hunger
of sadness. How's my father? He's not here.

Isn't home either. And mother's white silences
last too long—last an only brother's death too long.
And the priest pays us too many visits.
It seems my father has to stay with the police

because his accounting wasn't quite right.
And that he was ill then from not being home with us.
And now he has to stay over there until he is well.

Over there: seems to be jail.
Other boys go fishing with their fathers.
I have a father made ill from having had to miss me.

2.

Years later, I'm twenty, and I should know now,
and must understand that, well, it wasn't
easy for him, that he was not a homosexual,
but still, you know, just a tad pedophile.

And so that was why he'd spend some time in jail.
I'm four. Would I come next to him on the couch.
I must make believe I'm asleep. He does too.
All of a sudden I'm hundreds of thousands of tiny hairs.

All goosebumps is what it feels like to be me.
When it's over, I can still feel how straight up
they were, those tiny hairs, how many, one after the other.

Only now do I think: he tickled me—
hours of it—not to make me giggle,
but because he didn't dare stroke me.

Ann

I remember myself most. How, all of a sudden I had one
wife, instead of now and then this love or that.
And how we had to love each other, instead of simply
falling in love sometimes.

I used to sit in bars, boasting about how beautiful you were,
and shy, and brash too, until my women friends would say:
why don't you just go and be in love at home—
and how I still needed to order that one last drink.

I remember how silently you sat sometimes, hugging
your knees; how you wanted to be all sorts of women
for me, if only I'd be there.
And how, too young, I was unable to receive so much.

1971

I was better at losing: barely squeezed out
one poetry collection about it. I won
the Flemish Provinces Prize with your death.
I mostly remember I couldn't find my glasses.

They were on the road, next to the car. I found them
first, a new pair, then you.
Thanks to those glasses, I can still see you.
After an eternity, lasting

for a minute or two, a woman pointed to the grass:
look, a child. Oh, yes, we had that too. Quick mouth
to mouth. Tom howling as if murdered. That sounded healthy.

Only then did I realize how silent it had been before.
I thought: what if I tried to cry?
It worked. And that helped a lot in the following days.

for Thomas

Poetry

A painting needs a frame,
as happiness needs mortal fear.

Wind leafs through the garden
and suddenly a page
is turned. Like me ruffling your hair,
and how it lies differently now.

Yet nothing changes after all.
Look, says happiness, cradling this moment,
which shivers a little in its hands.

Snowmass Village

We sat on a rock in your garden,
looking out over the valley. There was so much below.
And much above: the Milky Way, the hereafter.

Of birth or death, you said—or did I—
the first remains the greatest wonder.

The stars, we were still very much under.
And us—the world could do without us.

for Laure-Anne

Paris, May 1st

in the Jewish war memorial

Paris, a hundred yards behind Notre Dame
a set of stairs descends into a strange underground chamber.
Down there a concrete wall, and in that a
gap, a tomb, and you can enter there

if you want to know how it feels to be dead with six million others.
You peer down a narrow hall, two mosaic walls,
each fifty yards long, each facet
an ode, a body. If it took each only ten minutes

to die you'd have a century. This one.
Up there it rains. Wind displaces gray.
A gull dishrags the sky, loses itself over the Seine:

across the street, twenty busloads of Le Pen.
I wish I was more of a stranger here than I am.
And this century less mine.

Gendray

The cow. How for centuries
she's stuck with the same plan.
Sort of like the Volkswagen Bug.
The never-changing cow-cow.
But here they lie—beautiful girls almost—
staring goddesses, their large
vacuum cleaner bellies fit to burst,
a tad aghast with mundane delight.
One of them, tired of all this lying work,
ponders how to stand upright.

"Hop, in the curtains, hop on the tabletop"

Hop, in the curtains, hop on the tabletop, hop
on my shoulder, hop on top of the keyboard:
kitty. Before I can ask myself
what I've done, I am condemned to just

look around, arrive too late everywhere, small sprints
zigzag through my life a second before I do,
and before it's over, it starts again,
no, kitty, not this key, that's Delete.

Little rusty-eyes. I'd love to have that looklooklook.
And with your quick paw, play ice hockey
with a match, pat, pat. And chase after

your tail. And be unable to catch yourself.
And want everything at once, then maybe not,
and fall asleep. Delete.

"Profession: inspector general of rhododendrons"

Profession: inspector general of rhododendrons,
star expert, self-appointed guardian of the literal
(except certain nights: reading Roald Dahl),
through-the-world driver, me and my gas pedal.

But in reality, I'm only wasting time
until you come home, so that I can say
nice-day-but-don't-go-out-again-OK-
and-do-you-still-love-me?

Planting sprouts in the sod, water
splitting them like syllables. Young buds,
they must promise you that they'll grow.

I see it before I can believe my eyes, my daughter
playing hide-and-seek in the garden: one-two-three...
Gotcha! she shouts to God.

Around and About

on an etching by Reinhoud

Someone whispered something
in the tiny ear between her legs.
So now she lies curled listening to it.
(*To remember* is the step after *to take in.*)

Two arms, like "around" and "about"
embracing the word "it."
The way water circles around a stone
in a rewound movie:

thc stone pulls the water about itself.

"What will you do today?"

—What will you do today? —Nothing.
—You already did that yesterday.
—No, that was a different kind of nothing.
(Zen: a bicycle works best when you let it stand, that's how

you get to where you already are.) Decided to grow
old. To start doing it now. When you're old
you don't enjoy it that much.
Final goal is to be a Zen poet. Ten lines a year.

Stare at a caterpillar until it almost
eats all the leaf it sits on. Let it crawl
on your finger. Then say, "Chomp it up,
little thing," and put it on another leaf.

Epithalamium

Choose me. Choose me out of the whole population
of the world. You can hesitate a little
about other guys,
but then choose me.

Worldly wisdom no one really wants,
old uncle Louie's jokes, rumors,
put your arms around this,
it's yours. You can have it all.

I'll get you, get to have you every day
and may even love your daughter.
Let's marry—all of us.

from *Fingerprints* (1997)

Fingerprints on a Window

I believe poetry is like fingerprints
on a window, behind which a child who can't sleep
stands waiting for dawn. Mist rises from the earth,

a sigh of sadness. Clouds
provide for twenty-five kinds of light.
In fact, they hold it back: backlight.

It's still too early to be now. But the rivers
are already leaving. They heard the hum
of the sea's silver factories.

My daughter stands next to me by the window. To love her
is the best way to remember all of this.
Birds find, in the forge of their sound, the word

gone, gone, gone.

Evening, Mid-May

Doors to the garden are open, odors
and mosquitoes waft in and out, the new leaves
of the weeping beech are counted, one hundred today,
uncountable tomorrow.

The blue flowered vine tries to climb
around a pole, something like the way a man—until
his forties—needs a penis to feel
he's getting around as well.

The young ginkgo is the most beautiful,
all those tiny hands at dawn
sharing one drop of dew and keeping it
in their palms all day.

Thank you, today, for still being here tonight,
for still holding on to now for a while.
It's all so much, a little bit
goes a long way to being everything.

Pointillism

A duckweed-filled ditch, pointillism
of green, stock-still shiver
of beginning, nature putting five billion
dots on its i's all at once.

Me on my belly by the ditch.
Hand me my glasses. Must check those dots. That's my job,
important enough to make me lie on my belly.
How many dots do you need for green?

How many grains, granules of sand to make a beach?
How many humans for humanity?
Two.
Someone with freckles, and someone to count them.

for Laura and Tom

November

Two leaves left hanging
on my maple. Thousands
blushed, thus died.
Forgot to look.

Forgot to be happy.
Although I had a garden,
which had a chair, and that chair
had me, and I had a hand

and that hand had a glass
and my mouth had meanings.
Everything had.
Everything had us.

"Slow snowing. As if it snowed upwards"

Slow snowing. As if it snowed upwards into
weightlessness. (That's how I rise with my syllables,
the way I sit, elevated a little, in the high thrones
of my lines.) Someone, God, holds his breath

and it snows into the vacuum. Primordial, suspended
explosion of whiteness. Bare tree a candelabrum
with three inches of snow on each of its inch-thick branches.
Like underlining. But *over*lining.

It's night. A storm, like the milky way, dances.
My garden gathers the flakes of that whiteness
the way a pointillist canvas still harbors
what was brought to it long ago:

an absence of gravity.

Last Post

I had to go to Ypres. It was around six.
I drove toward the setting sun and three-story-high
Dali-like clouds, chased away by nine-knot

winds, the sky was blown away from the earth,
I needed to let it go. I drove and drove, ninety mph,
but for each minute I drove I lost ten, stretching the horizon.

When I arrived in Ypres, it was 1917. The Germans had shot
the sun. No light left but explosions.
I find myself in a poem by Edmund Blunden.

From inside a trench, he writes an ode to poppies.
The earth is covered with a huge *Über-ich* of flowers.
Blunden sees them, literally, through his visor.

Here, the last second before you die
lasts for years.
There are only minutiae.

Later, at the Menin Gate memorial, I hear *The Last Post*:
three bugles slicing through what remains
of ninety years of marrow and bone.

"If all rivers were made of ink"

If all rivers were made of ink,
and all trees were pens,
one still couldn't write down
the suffering at Auschwitz.

Jakov Zilberberg said this
in the documentary *Ein Einfacher Mensch*;
he had belonged to the Sondercommando
who cremated the gassed cadavers.

For a whole hour, the documentary showed his eyes
over and over. The film stopped. But not those eyes.
He could no longer pass by a train station

without seeing bodies step out.
He could no longer speak without having to be quiet.
He could no longer look, or he saw.

May Evening, Gendray

How does it fall, evening?
(Like drizzle, but without the drizzle?)
A late maybug buzzes around, ponderous
flier. In the distance, a car vanishes beyond its noise.

Slowly, the colza-fields fade in their golden poise.
I hear milk pails clang in my uncle's
barn. The echo of white walls.
In a trough, piss lingers like Guinness,

dark and foamy. The last remnants of the day.
Minutes are over; here come the hours.
The present may exist now without meaning. Double wonder:
reality with, and without meaning any longer.

Father comes home from work. He brought someone along:
uncle Evening, who sits with me at the table. Visits.
After dinner, he'd like to read a book. Now and then,
he says yes, yes. Guess he's right,

he wrote it after all. It's about today.
When he's finished, he begins again.
—I'm startled awake: something's no longer here. The maybug.
I must have been dreaming. It's nine o'clock.

Night sits heavily by the hearth.
I hadn't seen it enter.

Ars Poetica

"Not much is needed to love here.
Someone says 'here' against the unmeasurable.

A coin on the mantle,
a passport photo. The unforgettable
is that small." End quote.

What originally stood there was:
the unforgettable is "that huge." I changed
it to "that small." It took me a year to do that.
A poet must work hard learning to be silent:

a gravestone listening to what is etched in it.
Letters that listen until they're filled with rain.

Acknowledgments

We wish to thank the editors of the following periodicals in which these translations, or versions of them, first appeared:

AGNI: Yonder

Circumference: Poetry

FIELD: "The way you came in and said hello"; "And she hugged him with all her sins"; The Rhinoceros; May Evening, Gendray

Georgia Review: Two Kinds of Nothing; "What a lack of pathos"; Sailor's Song

Harvard Review: "Just as this island belongs to the gulls"

Kestrel: "'Yes, sleep,' I say"; Defuser of Mines

Massachusetts Review: Genesis; Paris, May 1st

Nimrod: Juniper Tree, Canyonlands

91st Meridian: "If only he could, just like that, leave her"; Mother; Hérault

TriQuarterly: Pointillism; Around and About; "Hop, in the curtains, hop on the tabletop"; Epithalamium; "I come from far away"

About the Author

Herman de Coninck, Flanders' leading poet, was born in Mechelen on February 21, 1944, and died in 1997 in Lisbon, Portugal. For 13 years he worked as a journalist for the Flemish weekly *Humo*. In 1984, he founded *New World Magazine* (*Nieuwe Wereldtijdschrift*), which quickly became the most important Dutch literary review.

The author of seven highly acclaimed, prize-winning books of poetry in Dutch, he has also published two books of critical essays. Some of his poems have been translated into Polish, Chinese, Bulgarian, and German. Six poems were translated into English for the anthology *Dutch Interiors: Postwar Poetry of the Netherlands and Flanders*, edited by James Holmes and William Jay Smith (Columbia University Press). Posthumous volumes include *Collected Letters (1965-1997)*, *Collected Poetry*, and *Collected Prose*.

After losing his first wife in a car accident in 1971, Herman de Coninck was married to prize-winning novelist and short story writer Kristien Hemmerechts. The two lived and worked in Antwerp, Belgium, where Ms. Hemmerechts still resides.

About the Translators

Laure-Anne Bosselaar grew up in Belgium, where her first language was Dutch. She is the author of a book of poems in French, *Artemis* (1973), and two collections of poems in English from BOA, *The Hour Between Dog and Wolf* (1997) and *Small Gods of Grief* (2001), which won the Isabella Gardner Award for Poetry. She is also editor of *Outsiders: Poems about Rebels, Exiles and Renegades* (1999) and *Urban Nature: Poems about Wildlife in the City* (2000), both from Milkweed, as well as *Never Before: Poems about First Experiences* (Four Way Books, 2005). With her husband, she co-edited the anthology *Night Out: Poems about Hotels, Motels, Restaurants and Bars* (Milkweed, 1997).

Kurt Brown is the editor of *Drive, They Said: Poems about Americans and Their Cars* (1994) and *Verse & Universe: Poems about Science and Mathematics* (1998), both from Milkweed. He is also co-editor, with his wife, of *Night Out*. In addition, he has edited three books of lectures delivered at writers' conferences: *The True Subject* (Graywolf, 1993), *Writing It Down for James* (Beacon, 1995) and *Facing the Lion* (Beacon, 1996), as well as *The Measured Word: On Poetry and Science* (Georgia, 2001). He has published three collections of poems: *Return of the Prodigals* (1999) and *More Things in Heaven and Earth* (2002), both from Four Way Books, and *Fables from the Ark*, which won the 2003 Custom Words Prize (WordTech, 2003). A fourth, *Future Ship*, will appear from Red Hen Press in 2007.